The Little Gray Digger

written by
Sonica Ellis

Illustrated by
Harriet Rodis

DEDICATION

This book is dedicated to Bernard Kochczynski.
Don't ever change who you are to fit in with the crowd.
Always be yourself because you are amazing just the way you are!

Love always and forever!

Sonnie

ISBN: 978-0-578-79670-3

Copyright © 2020
All Rights Reserved

There was once a town called Builderville, and in Builderville, everyone worked together to build things.

There was Billy Bob the Backhoe,

Carl the Crane,

Fiona the Forklift,

Danny the Dumptruck,

and Bernie the Bulldozer.

One morning, they were all hard at work building a library when someone new arrived to join the crew. It was a little digger named Scoop.

"Hi, my name is Bernie. What's yours?" asked Bernie with a smile. Scoop looked at Bernie and replied, "My name is Scoop."
"Nice to meet you, Scoop. Come on, I'll introduce you to the others."

But as Scoop made his way to meet the others, he could hear them talking among themselves.

Scoop was not the same as the others, you see. While all the others were yellow, Scoop was gray.

Being different made Scoop feel very uncomfortable.

Scoop thought that if he looked like everyone else, he would feel much better. Then, others might stop talking about him.

This gave Scoop an idea!

The next day, Scoop stopped by the Builderville hardware store, where he bought three big cans of yellow paint and two paintbrushes.

He asked Bernie for help to paint himself yellow.

"Are you sure you want to do this, Scoop?" Bernie asked. "You know I love you just as you are. I'll always be your friend, whether you're gray, yellow, or even pink!"

"I know," said Scoop, "but I just want to be like everyone else."

And so, they painted Scoop yellow.

Not long after they had finished, it began to rain, and all the paint washed off.

Scoop was gray once more.

Scoop was disappointed, but soon he had another idea.

"Maybe if I wear yellow clothes to hide my gray, the others won't talk about me."

Using his mother's sewing machine, some old clothes, sheets, and a bright yellow raincoat, Scoop created something that would cover him up.

Although he looked quite funny, he was yellow.

"Besides, it is not what you look like on the outside that counts, it's what's on the inside that matters."

Before Scoop could say anything, he heard a voice from above.

"He's right, you know, I have to say. What's so wrong with being gray?"

asked a nightingale, which was perched overhead in a nearby tree.

"Redbirds and Blue Jays, it's true to say, sing beautifully most every day.

But I am gray, and to hear me sing is as beautiful as anything!"

"I just want to fit in!" cried Scoop.

"I think it would be a great shame if everyone looked just the same.

You be you, and I'll be me. It's much more fun, I think you'll see."

Scoop listened very closely as the nightingale continued.

"Being you is a superpower,
like sunlight to the growing flower.

Love yourself each day and week,
and be proud that you're unique!"

"You are right, Ms. Nightingale," replied Scoop, feeling much better.

With newfound confidence, Scoop removed the old sheets and clothes covering him.

He went over to the others, who were gathered around the site.

"My name is Scoop," he said proudly.
"I am a little gray digger, and that is fine by me!"

The End

Library
UNDER
CONSTRUCTION

Lesson Plan - Self-acceptance

Learning Intention and Success Criteria

Learning Intention
- We are learning about self-acceptance.

Success Criteria:
I will be successful when I can:
- Understand what self-acceptance means.
- Recognize that everyone is different.
- Show that I am proud of my differences.
- Accept my differences and love myself for who I am.

Resources

- The Little Gray Digger: A Book About Insecurity" story
- Self-acceptance worksheet (PDF or editable PowerPoint version)
- Colored pencils

Mini Lesson

Connector: Students are to listen to "The Little Gray Digger: A Book About Insecurity" story read aloud by the teacher. After the teacher has read the story to the students, ask the students:
1. Why was Scoop trying to change the way he looked?
2. Do you think Benny was right when he told Scoop that it would be a shame if everyone looked the same? Why do you think he said that to Scoop?
3. How do you think Scoop felt when he decided to accept that he was different?

The teacher is to discuss that everyone is different in their own way and we should all be proud of the way we are. The teacher is to also discuss that we need to accept ourselves for who we are.

The students are to turn and talk to another student and discuss what is different about them. After the partner discussion, the students are to share back with the class. The teacher is to show students that everyone is different and that is something we need to be proud of.

The teacher is to model how to complete the self-acceptance worksheet. The teacher is to give an example by drawing themselves on the mirror. The teacher is to also model writing a sentence to show what difference they have that they are proud of. *For example, "I am proud of wearing my red glasses."*

Independent Task

The students are to complete this worksheet either on the hardcopy or the PowerPoint presentation file of self-acceptance worksheet. The students are to draw themselves in the mirror. Then they are to write a sentence about a difference they are proud of.

To cater to all needs of your students, adjust the task using the modifications below:

Support: Students can draw themselves in the mirror on the worksheet.
Extension: After completing the worksheet, the students are to write why they are proud of their differences.

Reflection

The students are to share their worksheet with the whole class and what differences they have that they are now proud of.

Download lesson plan at https://drive.google.com/file/d/1PQ9zIh51GLmBLVRDbrU2VPipOUUOeh10/view?usp=sharing

Name_____   Date_____

I Am Proud of Who I Am!

Draw yourself in the mirror

I see someone who is...

I am proud of _____

Made in the USA
Monee, IL
29 August 2021